Why Do We Fly Paper Airplanes?

A paper airplane symbolizes freedom. To soar above the earth, floating on a current of air like a bird in flight, is a hope that lives inside us all, young and old. Since ancient times, man has dreamt of imitating the beating wings of a bird. We have made great advances in powered flight, yet the paper airplane a simple, wing-shaped, human-powered toy still embodies the age-old desire to fly. This book presents paper plane designs from around the globe, ranging from easy gliders for the beginner to challenging flights of fancy for the experienced aero-engineer. Once you have mastered the basics, you might want to try designing your own planes, or creating games and competitions. The sky is the limit!

Don't worry. To be a master, you will make plenty of these.

Get ready to fold your way to being a master paper airplane flyer.

GOOD LUCK!

3

Off to a Flying Start

Paper and Folding Instructions

Each awesome paper airplane in this book requires only a single sheet of paper. No cutting, taping, or gluing needed. Practice each design with a plain sheet of paper, before using the printed sheets provided in the back of the book. This way, if you make a mistake, its not with the good stuff.

Keep the paper flat or in the plastic sleeve until you're ready to use it. Always start with Side 1 up (see diagram below). To see which side is side one, check the paper symbol located at the top of each page. Match the colored paper design to the correct airplane design.

 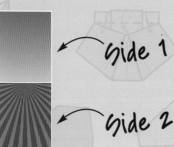

Side 1

Side 2

Types of Paper

Once you have used all the colored paper provided, try experimenting with different papers. Avoid using paper that is too heavy (construction paper, watercolor paper, drawing paper) or too light (tissue paper, paper towels, tissue). Photocopy paper is the ideal weight and thickness and comes in an array of colors. Unusual papers you might want to consider include patterned wrapping paper, junk mail, paper-backed metallic, quality color magazine paper, disposable table cloths, thin tracing paper, and lightweight homemade paper.

Note: When not folding airplanes, store paper horizontally and flat, away from humid or damp air. Throw away any sheets that have bent corners or crescent-shaped buckle marks, unless you know the damaged areas will be buried deep inside the layers of the nose, where they cannot disturb the smooth airflow over the paper's surface.

For the best flying results, make sure the right side and the left side mirror each other when folding. The slightest mistake can make a big difference.

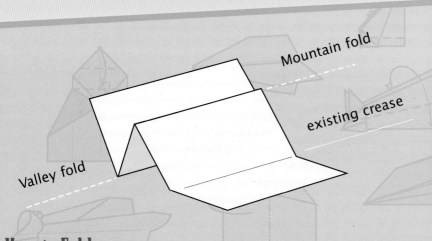

Mountain fold

existing crease

Valley fold

How to Fold

Always fold on a hard surface, such as a tabletop or a large hardback book, and make sharp creases—never fold entirely in the air, on your lap, or using a soft surface, such as a carpet. The first drawing of each plane shows an existing crease, or creases, that divide the paper in half or quarters. Fold neatly and accurately, making sure that edges or corners meet exactly as indicated. Smooth the layers flat after each step.

Symbols

The symbols in this book are commonly used in paper plane books throughout the world. The most important thing to understand is the difference between a Mountain fold and a Valley fold. Each step builds on the other, so keep looking ahead to see the results of what you are doing now. Refer to this guide whenever you run into an unfamiliar symbol.

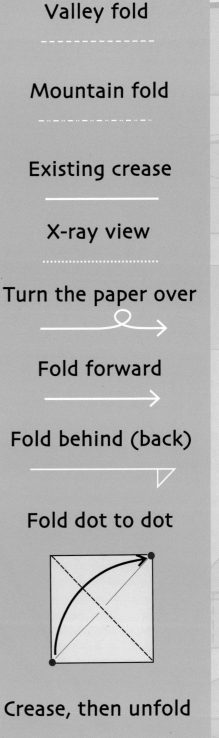

Valley fold

Mountain fold

Existing crease

X-ray view

Turn the paper over

Fold forward

Fold behind (back)

Fold dot to dot

Crease, then unfold

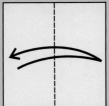

Off to a Flying Start

Flying Tips

Tweaking

Experiencing a failure to launch? First off, think of the first throw as a test to see how well the airplane performs. Does it nosedive, stall, dive-bomb, or barrel-roll? Once you've identified the problem, you can try to solve it. However, keep in mind that planes are fickle. A plane that dives for one person may stall when somebody else throws it, or a glider that sails majestically into the distance on the first throw may never do it again. There are some reliable ways to improve performance, usually involving the perfect combination of trimming and launching. Adjusting the angle the wings make across the top of the fuselage is a good place to start. Checking the symmetry, elevators (which make the plane go up and down), and ailerons (which make plane bank or roll) are other tweaking methods.

Safety Tip:
Never throw a plane directly at another person, especially if the plane has a sharp, pointed nose.

Speed

Novice plane fliers tend to throw a paper plane either too softly, so it never catches the air and wafts drowsily to the ground, or with so much force it barrels rapidly through the air before meeting a violent end. Most planes do best with moderate force, although experimenting with different speeds can yield successful results.

Throwing angles

The four main angles of launch are vertically upward, diagonally upward, horizontal, and downward. Vertically upward requires speed and athleticism, as the intention is to hurl the plane as high as possible before it starts to level out and begin its stately descent. Diagonally upward at an angle between 30 degrees and 45 degrees is the most familiar and versatile launch, especially at moderate speeds. Play around with the precise angle of launch—too steep can make the plane stall, too shallow can reduce the distance or length of the flight. Horizontal launching results in steady, unassuming flights and is best for delicate gliders in limited spaces. Downward launching may seem like a kamikaze mission, but it can create spectacular acrobatic flights. Always throw downward launches with great speed, and never gently.

Indoors/Outdoors

Darts and slow gliders are ideal for the indoor's calm air and confined space. Outdoors, hardier, heavier planes make the best fliers, but small darts and high-flying gliders are also ace performers.

Off to a Flying Start

Flying Guide

Darts

These planes are built for distance and speed. They are sleek and streamlined, not a wasted angle. Throw dart planes straight or at an upward, 45-degree angle, and launch it like you mean it. A hard throw is the best throw.

Remember! If the plane has narrow wings throw the plane harder. If the plane has wide wings throw the plane softer.

Not all Dart planes will have the pointed nose tip.

Darts fly best when thrown within this angle range

Gliders

The name says it all: gliders drift on streams of air. They fly long and slow, making wide, lazy turns and rarely land without gently bumping into something first. Most gliders are room-crossers, and can be launched with a smooth, even motion—remember, you are guiding the plane, not throwing it. On the other hand, high flier gliders are launched like a rocket—straight up, as if trying to poke a hole in the moon.

Gliders fly best when thrown within this angle range

Stunt planes fly best when thrown within these angle ranges

Stunt

Stunt planes are the barnstormers of the paper airplane world and the hardest working aircraft in the business—looping, circling, diving, and rolling and then coming back for more! Stunt planes can be thrown all sorts of ways, but the best method is with a medium-strength throw that is up and away from your body.

History of Paper Airplanes

Paper planes are a form of aerogami, a variation on origami, the Japanese art of paper folding. Although no one has pinpointed exactly when the first tiny glider sailed through the air, using paper to create toys has been around for at least 2,000 years, when kites were a popular form of entertainment in China. In the Renaissance era, Leonardo da Vinci built a model airplane out of parchment, and in the late 1700s, the early model balloons from France's Montgofier Brothers were all made of paper. The inventor of model gliders is said to have been George Cayley, who built hand-launched, kite-like gliders from linen in the early 1800s.

While it is rumored the Wright Brothers experimented with paper models, the earliest known date of using paper airplanes to test aerodynamics was said to have been in 1909. Two decades later, Jack Northrup, cofounder of the Lockheed Corporation, widely used paper airplanes to try out ideas for flying real-life aircraft. In 1944, model paper airplane designs were offered by General Mills Corporation for two Wheaties® cereal box tops and the princely sum of five cents. Since WWII, paper airplanes have introduced millions of kids and adults to the pleasures of building models and flying their creations.

PAPER AIRPLANES RULE!

Are you ready to make paper airplanes?

Remember...this is Side One.

Eastern Star

A stellar model that glides perfectly. This glider requires a gentle throw that starts by holding the plane midway under the wings.

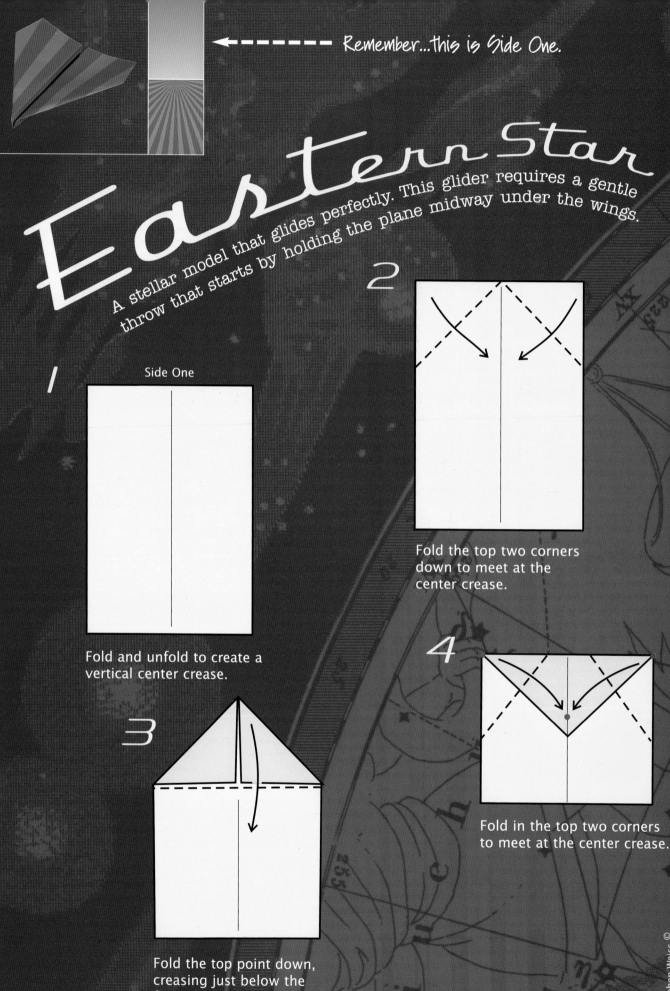

1 Side One

Fold and unfold to create a vertical center crease.

2 Fold the top two corners down to meet at the center crease.

3 Fold the top point down, creasing just below the flap edges.

4 Fold in the top two corners to meet at the center crease.

5

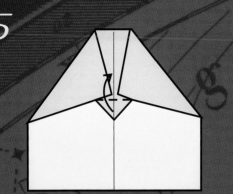

Fold the middle point up to
the center crease.

6

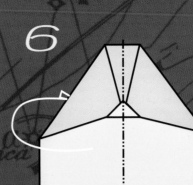

Mountain fold the plane
in half.

7

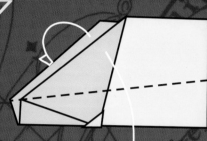

Fold both wings down.

TIP:
Horizontal launching
results in steady
flights and is best
for delicate gliders.

8

Ready for flight!

Type of plane: glider

Plane Name: Fly Paper

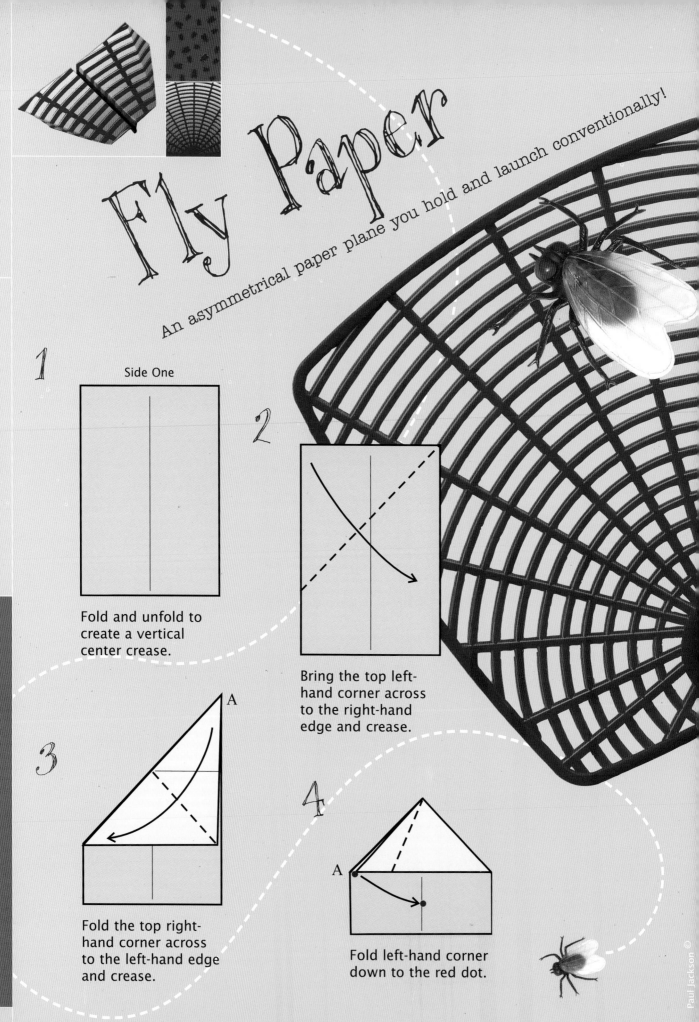

Fly Paper

An asymmetrical paper plane you hold and launch conventionally!

1

Side One

Fold and unfold to create a vertical center crease.

2

Bring the top left-hand corner across to the right-hand edge and crease.

3

A

Fold the top right-hand corner across to the left-hand edge and crease.

4

A

Fold left-hand corner down to the red dot.

14

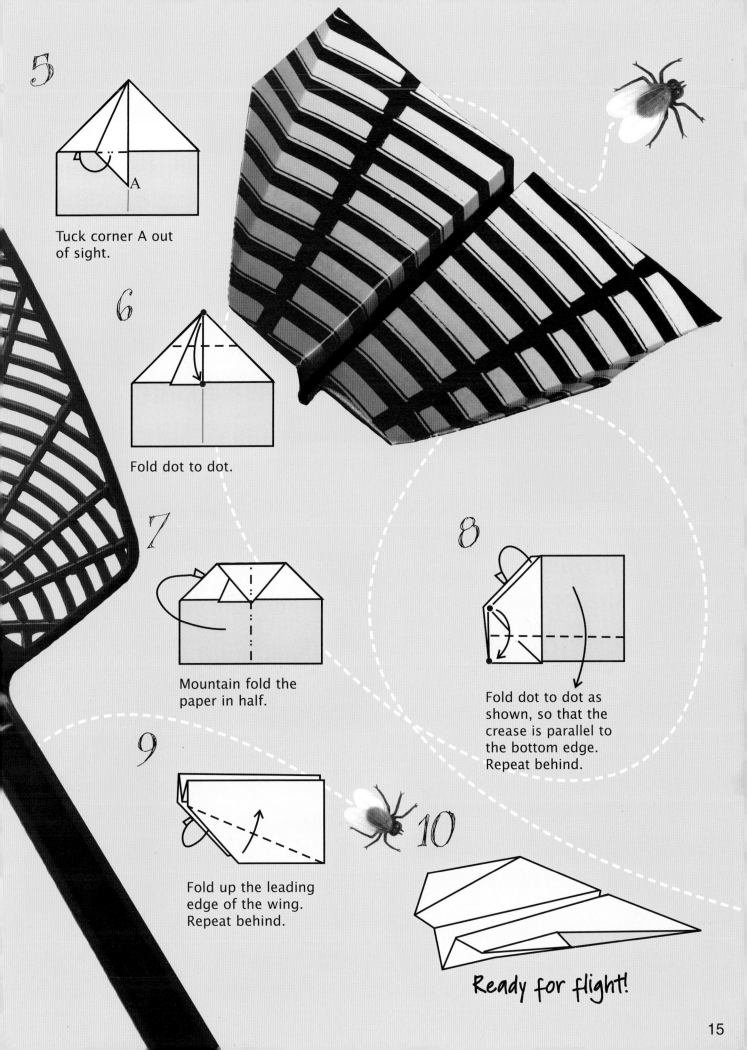

5

Tuck corner A out of sight.

6

Fold dot to dot.

7

Mountain fold the paper in half.

8

Fold dot to dot as shown, so that the crease is parallel to the bottom edge. Repeat behind.

9

Fold up the leading edge of the wing. Repeat behind.

10

Ready for flight!

triumph

this indoor and outdoor flier boasts a clean and elegant design.

1

Side One

Fold and unfold to create a vertical center crease.

2

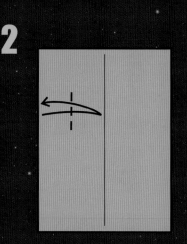

Crease and unfold.

3

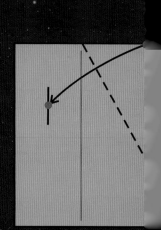

Fold right corner down, dot to dot.

4

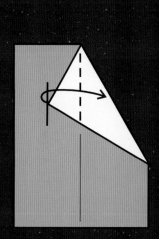

Valley fold flap to right edge of paper.

5

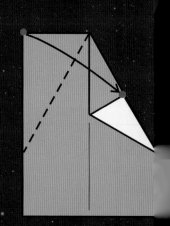

Valley fold top left corner down, dot to dot.

6

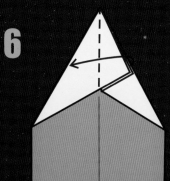

Fold top layer over to left edge of paper.

7

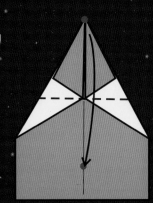

Fold tip of paper down, dot to dot.

8

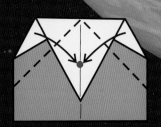

Fold down sides to meet at the red dot.

9

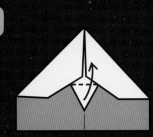

Fold small point in the middle up over side flaps.

10

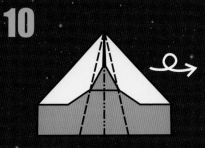

Pleat as shown and turn the plane over.

11

Ready for flight.

A54

Triumph

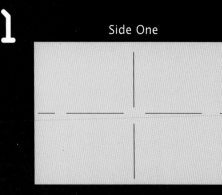

Delta Wing

Its simple triangular shape flies high!

1

Side One

Fold and unfold to create both vertical and horizontal center creases.

2

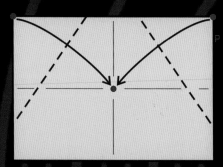

Fold the top corners down to meet at the center red dot.

3

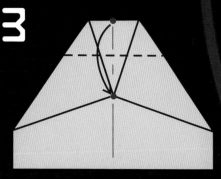

Valley fold down, dot to dot.

4

Fold down top corners to meet at the center crease.

5

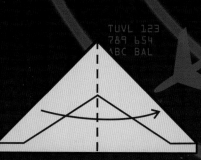

Valley fold the plane vertically in half.

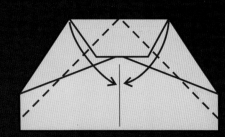

18

Paul Jackson ©

6

Horizontally fold the wing down at the reference line. Repeat for opposite side.

TIP:
Make sure you fold Steps 5 to 7 carefully and throw the plane with moderate force.

7

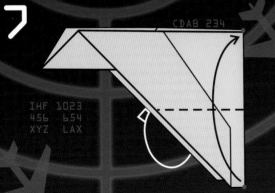

CDAB 234

IHF 1023
456 654
XYZ LAX

Fold tip of wing up, dot to dot. Repeat for opposite side.

8

Ready for flight!

WISK WING

A GRACEFUL FLIER, WHETHER INSIDE OR OUTDOORS.

1

Side One

Fold and unfold to create a vertical center crease.

2

Bring the top right corner down to the center of the bottom edge (do not crease entire edge) and make a short crease mark diagonally across the vertical centerline.

3

Fold down the top edge at the reference line, crease and then unfold.

TIP:
Put a finger inside each wing to separate and bow layers.

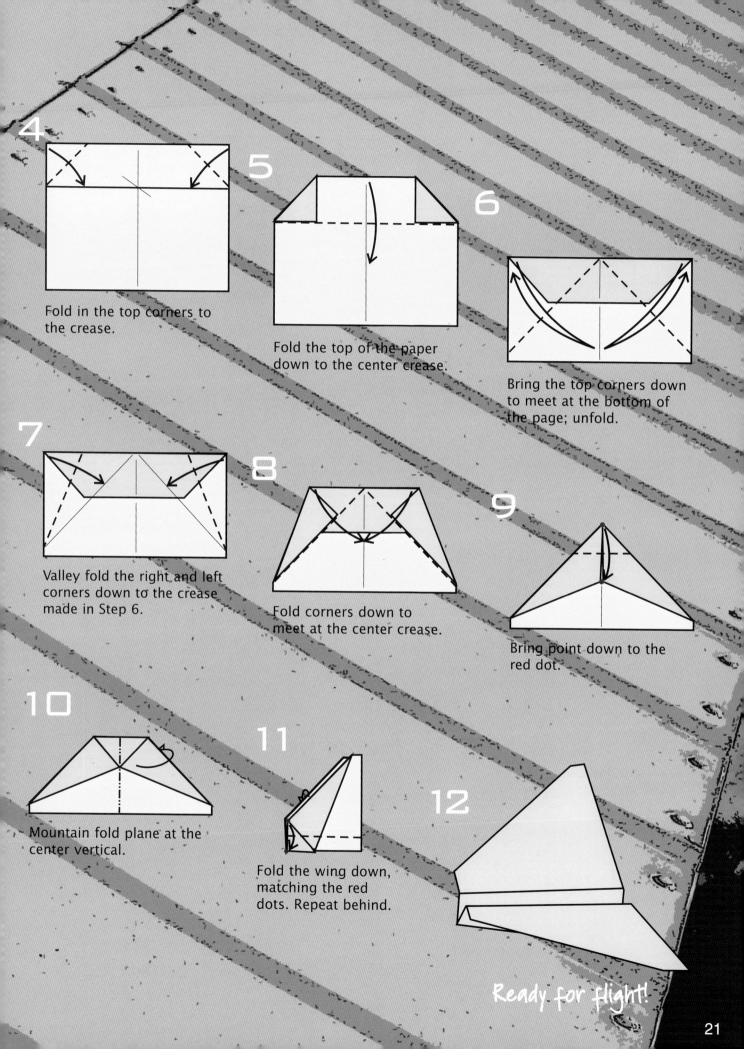

4 Fold in the top corners to the crease.

5 Fold the top of the paper down to the center crease.

6 Bring the top corners down to meet at the bottom of the page; unfold.

7 Valley fold the right and left corners down to the crease made in Step 6.

8 Fold corners down to meet at the center crease.

9 Bring point down to the red dot.

10 Mountain fold plane at the center vertical.

11 Fold the wing down, matching the red dots. Repeat behind.

12 Ready for flight!

CANARD

THIS TYPE OF PLANE HAS A STABILIZER IN FRONT OF THE WINGS.

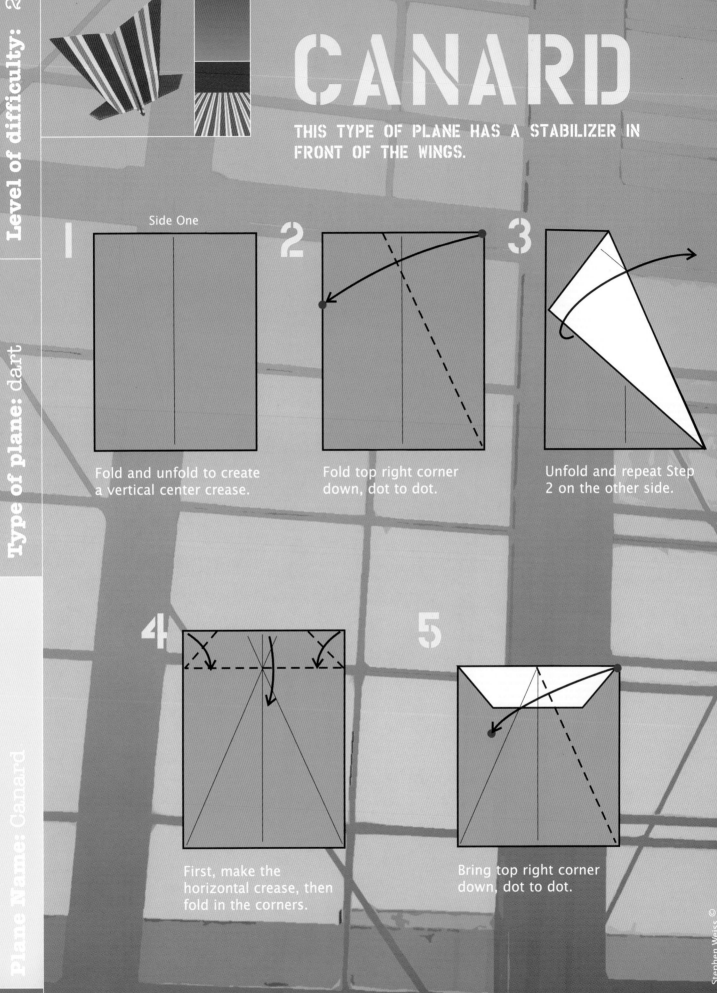

Side One

1 Fold and unfold to create a vertical center crease.

2 Fold top right corner down, dot to dot.

3 Unfold and repeat Step 2 on the other side.

4 First, make the horizontal crease, then fold in the corners.

5 Bring top right corner down, dot to dot.

6 Valley fold top layer to the right.

7 Repeat steps 5 and 6 on the other side.

8 Valley fold, dot to dot.

9 Mountain fold the plane in half.

10 Valley fold the wings down, dot to dot.

11 Ready for flight!

Troubleshooting Techniques

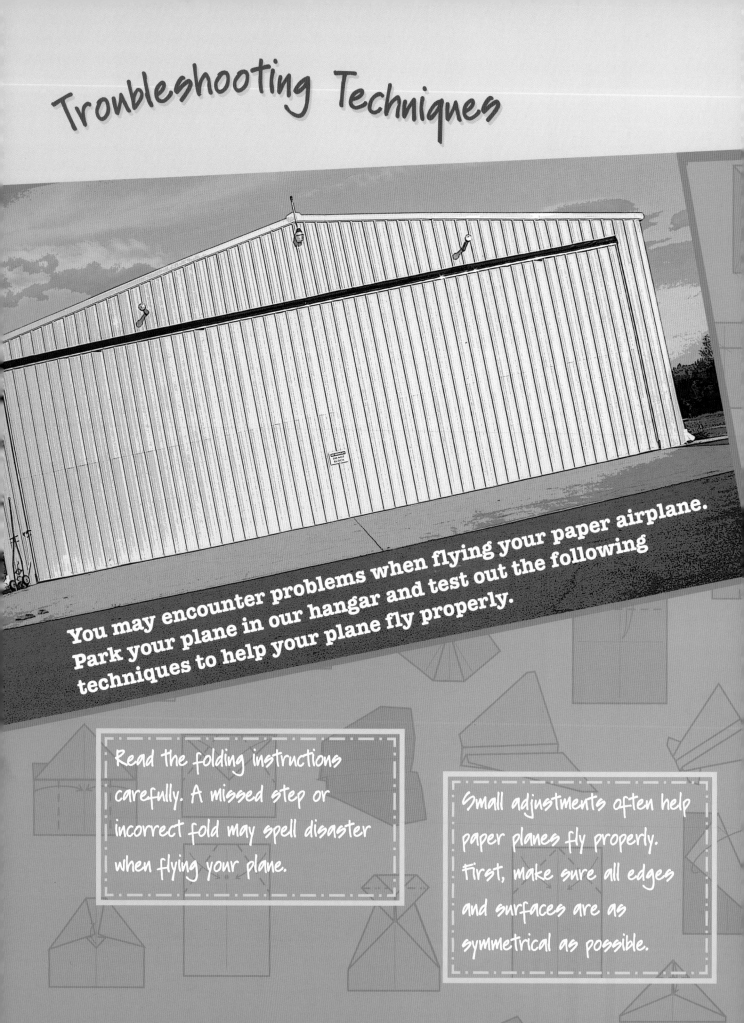

You may encounter problems when flying your paper airplane. Park your plane in our hangar and test out the following techniques to help your plane fly properly.

Read the folding instructions carefully. A missed step or incorrect fold may spell disaster when flying your plane.

Small adjustments often help paper planes fly properly. First, make sure all edges and surfaces are as symmetrical as possible.

If the plane rises, stalls, and drops, try curving the rear edges or corners slightly downward.

If a plane nose dives into the ground, try curving the rear edges or corners slightly upward.

Some planes fly better with a soft throw, while others need a harder throw, and some models can be thrown either way. An outdoor breeze may be all some planes need to become airborne.

Raising or lowering the wings evenly on both sides can also affect flight.

COMPASS

If all of your tweaking still results in a wobbly flight, try refolding it with a new sheet of paper.

33 0 3 6

30 9

27 12

SKY BARGE

THE CLEAN AND EFFICIENT DESIGN YIELDS SMOOTH, PLEASING FLIGHTS.

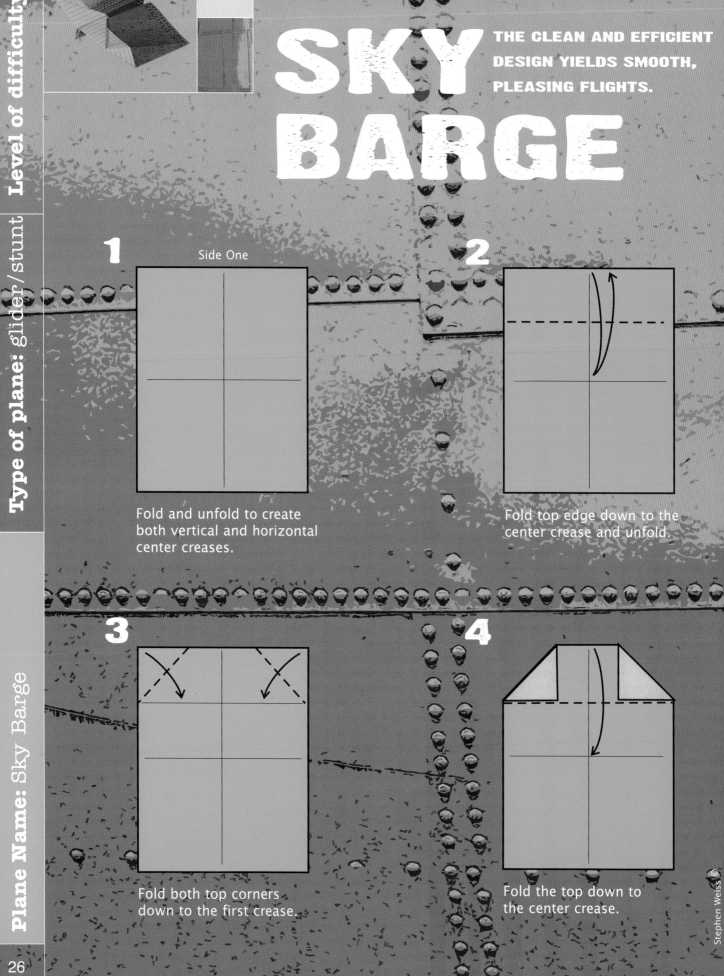

1 Side One

Fold and unfold to create both vertical and horizontal center creases.

2

Fold top edge down to the center crease and unfold.

3

Fold both top corners down to the first crease.

4

Fold the top down to the center crease.

Stephen Weiss ©

5

Fold both top corners down to meet at the middle crease.

6

Fold the top point down along the hidden edge (X-ray line).

7

Form the final shape. The side flaps should be bent down at 90 degrees to the wings.

Front View

8

Ready for flight!

hoop-nosed scooter

unusual in looks, but steady in performance.

1 Side One

Fold and unfold to create a vertical center crease.

2 A B
C D

Fold corners A and B in to center crease. Then, flip paper over.

3 B A
D C

Unfold corners A and B. Fold C and D in to center crease.

4 B A
D C

Valley fold top point down.

Paul Jackson ©

28

5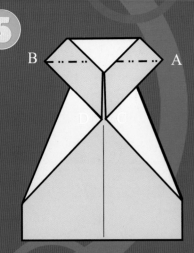

Valley fold at corners A and B.

6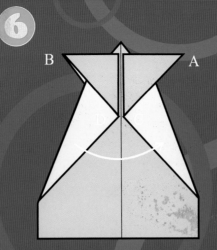

Valley fold the plane in half.

7

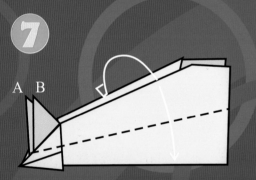

Fold the wing down. Repeat behind.

TIP:
Good flight depends on careful adjustment of the trailing edges, which usually need a slight upward bend.

8

A

B

Tuck corner A inside corner B to form a hoop.

9

Ready for flight!

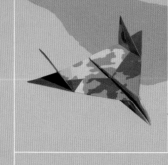

Thunder Bomber

A traditional design that's simple to fold and easy to fly, what could be better?

1

Side One

Fold and unfold to create a vertical center crease.

2

Fold the paper down horizontally.

3

Create two Squash folds. Note the positioning of the Valley folds. Press down and flatten the top edges at the arrows above.

4

Using Mountain folds, narrow the open ends of the Squash folds by folding under.

TIP:
Create Squash folds by first creasing and uncreasing the Valley folds. Then, press down and flatten the top edges.

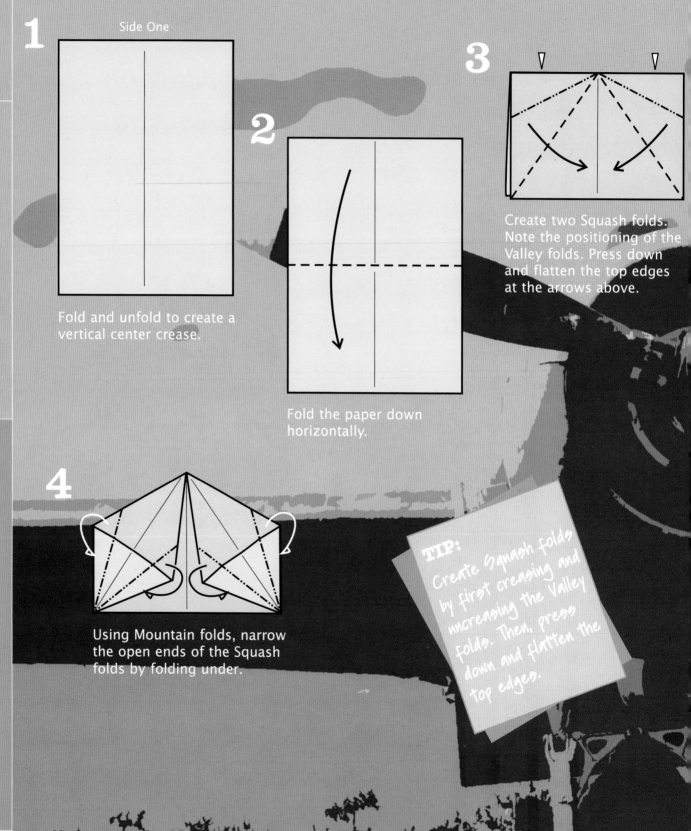

5

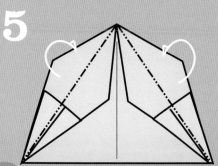

Fold the Squash folds in half.
The paper will be identically
folded, front and back.

6

Valley fold the paper in half.

7

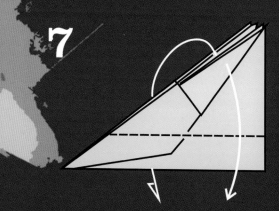

Valley fold both wings
downward.

8

Fold the top layer of
the wings upward.

9

Lift the wings up to the
horizontal.

10

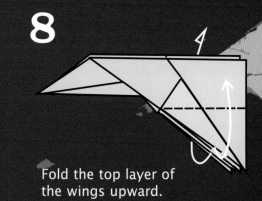

Ready for flight!

Type of plane: dart

Plane Name: Bull's-Eye Dart

BULL'S-EYE DART
THIS IS A GREAT PLANE FOR TARGET GAMES.

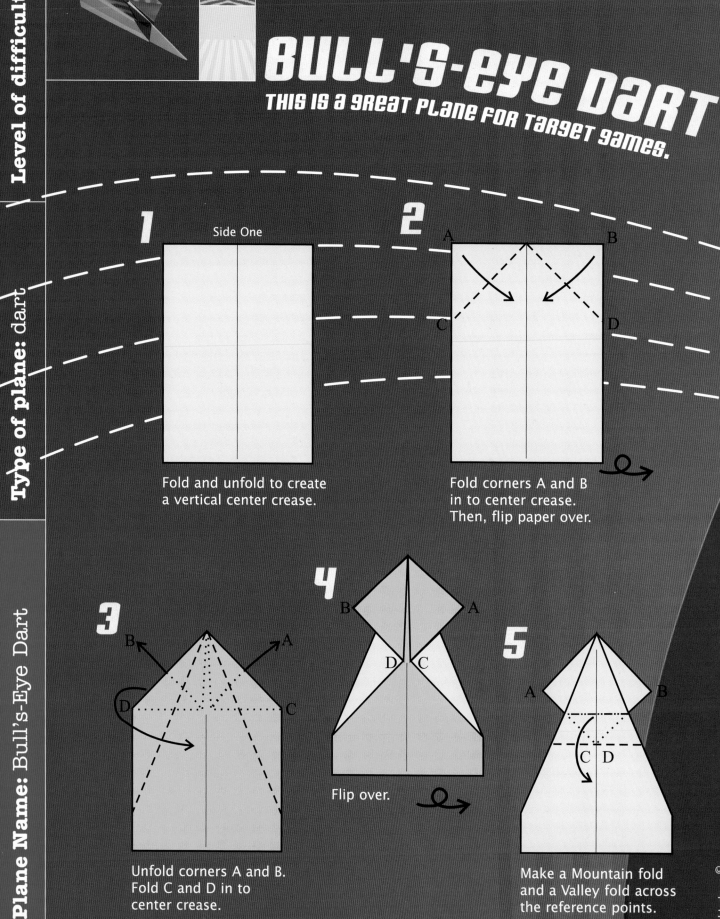

1 Side One

Fold and unfold to create a vertical center crease.

2

A · · · · · · · · · · B

C · · · · · · · · · · D

Fold corners A and B in to center crease. Then, flip paper over.

3

B ← · · · ↗ A

D · · · · · C

Unfold corners A and B. Fold C and D in to center crease.

4

B · · · A

D | C

Flip over.

5

A · · · B

C | D

Make a Mountain fold and a Valley fold across the reference points.

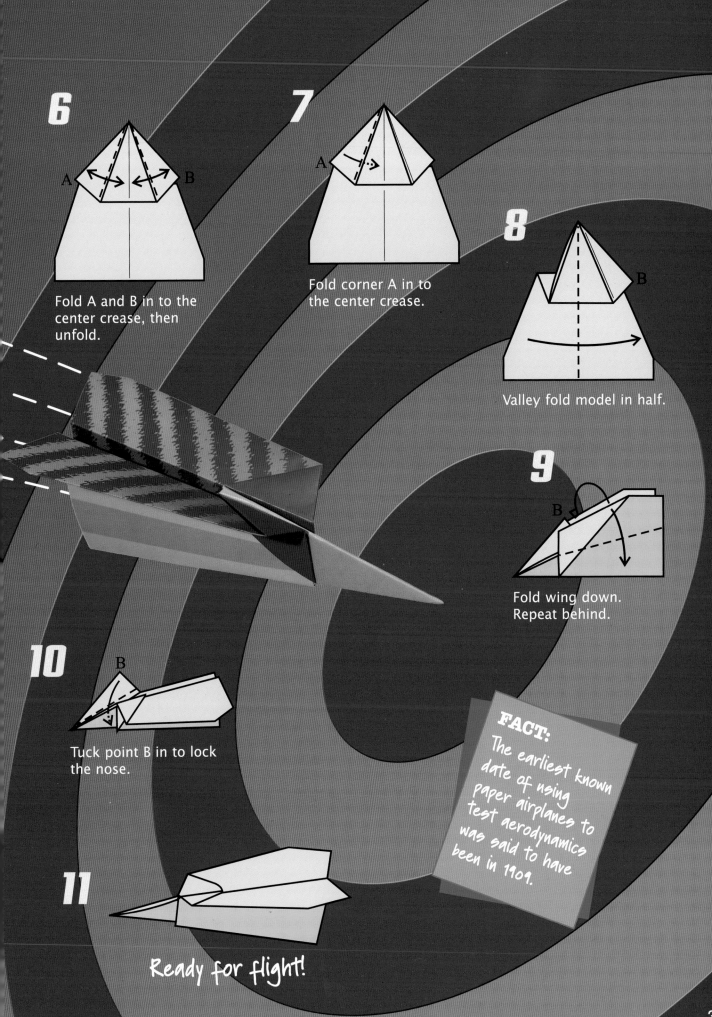

6

Fold A and B in to the center crease, then unfold.

7

Fold corner A in to the center crease.

8

Valley fold model in half.

9

Fold wing down. Repeat behind.

10

Tuck point B in to lock the nose.

11

Ready for flight!

FACT:
The earliest known date of using paper airplanes to test aerodynamics was said to have been in 1909.

FLAT FLYER

You'll get stable and fast flights if you throw it correctly.

1

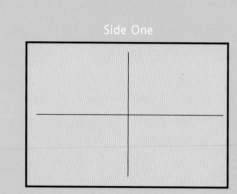

Side One

Fold and unfold to create both vertical and horizontal center creases.

2

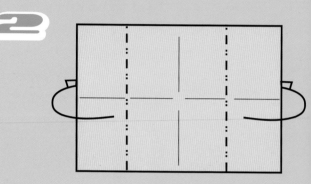

Mountain fold right and left sides to the center crease.

3

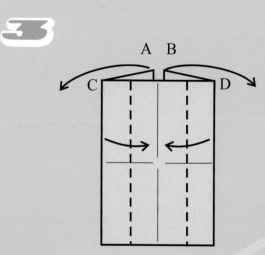

Turn in right and left sides at C and D to meet at center crease. Corners A and B will become new corners.

4

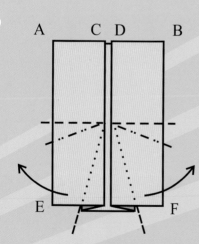

Pull corners E and F up and out, creating Mountain folds on both sides.

5

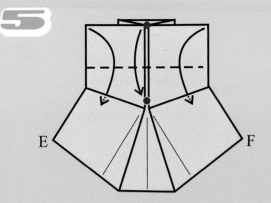

E   F

Fold down, dot to dot,
tucking corners under folds.

6

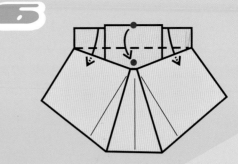

Fold again, tucking corners
behind folds.

7

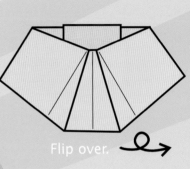

Flip over.

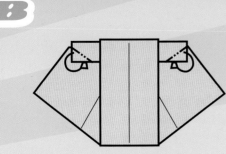

8

Tuck tips under.

9

Hold from this end.
Place your middle finger
on top and your first and
third finger underneath.
Launch forward.

Ready for flight!

interceptor

A sleek flier that travels straight and stays horizontal throughout its flight.

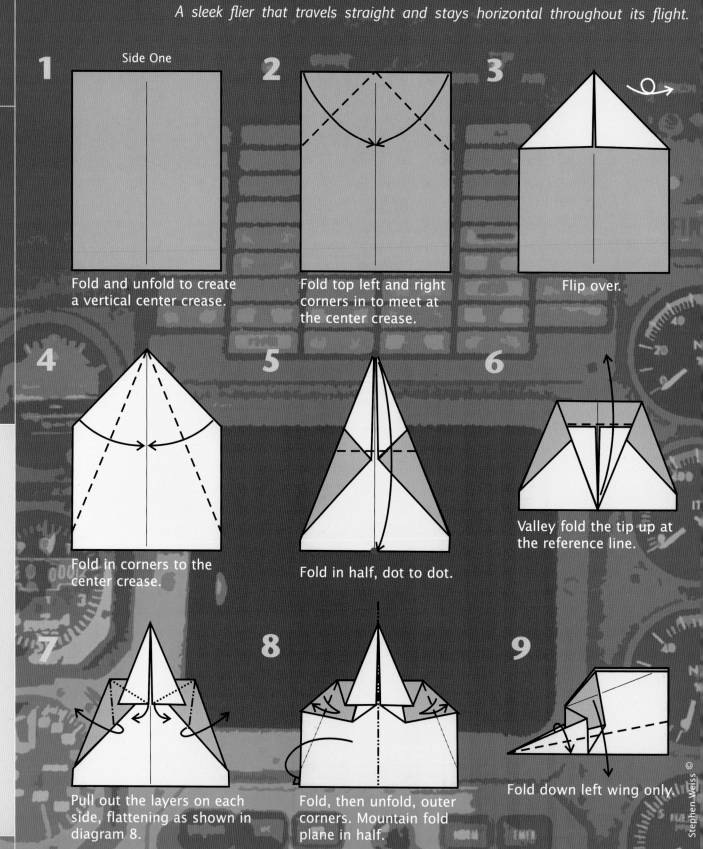

1 Side One

Fold and unfold to create a vertical center crease.

2

Fold top left and right corners in to meet at the center crease.

3

Flip over.

4

Fold in corners to the center crease.

5

Fold in half, dot to dot.

6

Valley fold the tip up at the reference line.

7

Pull out the layers on each side, flattening as shown in diagram 8.

8

Fold, then unfold, outer corners. Mountain fold plane in half.

9

Fold down left wing only.

Stephen Weiss ©

36

10

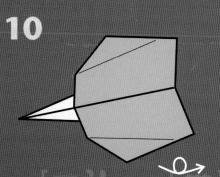

Flip over horizontally.

11

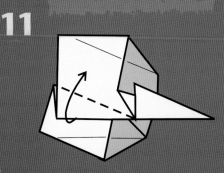

Crease bottom of plane up.

12

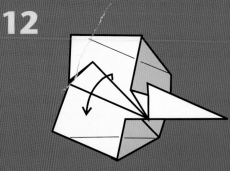

Crease bottom of plane down in the opposite direction.

13

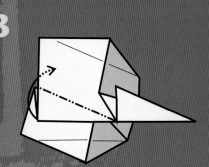

Reverse fold the tail by pushing the corner up along the creases made in Steps 11 and 12, turning it inside out.

14

While the plane is lying down flat as shown above, Valley fold the right wing down.

15

Fold the top corner of the tail over, tucking it into the body as far as possible.

16

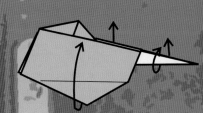

Raise and adjust wings.

17

Front view.

Ready for flight!

Flight Test

After folding and creating the 12 different paper airplanes, test them and see how they fly. Throw them hard or soft, high or low, try them in all sorts of ways and see what tricks get them to fly their best. Fill out the chart below to keep a record of your flight statistics.

Plane Name	Plane Type	Distance Traveled			Time in Flight			Favorite plane on a scale from 1 to 10
		First throw attempt	Second throw attempt	Third throw attempt	First throw attempt	Second throw attempt	Third throw attempt	
Eastern Star								
Fly Paper								
Triumph								
Delta Wing								
Wisk Wing								
Canard								
Sky Barge								
Hoop-Nosed Scooter								
Thunder Bomber								
Bull's-Eye Dart								
Flat Flyer								
Interceptor								